# The Stewardship Series 3

# GIFTS FROM THE HEART

## Giving to God What Belongs to God

The Stewardship Series 3

# GIFTS FROM THE HEART

## Giving to God What Belongs to God

## LARRY BURKETT

Edited by Adeline Griffith, Christian Financial Concepts

ISBN: 0-8024-2806-1

1 3 5 7 9 10 8 6 4 2

*Printed in the United States of America*

# TABLE OF CONTENTS

Using This Study Guide     7

**SESSION 1:** Freely You Have Received     11

**SESSION 2:** The Grace of Giving     23

**SESSION 3:** Giving to Receive     33

**SESSION 4:** Freely Give     45

**SESSION 5:** Widening the Circle     53

**SESSION 6:** Getting Organized     63

**SESSION 7:** Courageous Giving     71

# USING THIS STUDY GUIDE

Learning to handle money and possessions is one of the most important things we can do for our spiritual growth. Our use of money both reflects and greatly affects the true state of our relationship with God. But money is a touchy subject—rarely discussed in either pulpits or small groups—so many people are simply unaware of how much insight the Bible offers into handling money wisely.

The Stewardship Series of study guides is designed to help you learn and practice the basic biblical principles of handling wealth, whether you have a lot or a very little. A *steward* is someone who manages another person's property; God has entrusted every one of us with resources to manage for His purposes. When we understand God's goals and methods, managing money can become an exciting adventure instead of a confusing burden.

*Gifts from the Heart* addresses giving and tithing. Many of us feel guilty for not giving enough or are resentful of all the requests for money we receive. This study will explore good and bad reasons for giving, to whom we should give, and why and how we can afford it.

This guide is designed with small groups in mind. Money is an intensely private matter, and you won't be asked to divulge information inappropriately, but teaming up with a group of like-minded people offers you the chance to learn from others and receive their encouragement. However, you can easily adapt *Gifts from the Heart* for use with just one other person, or you can use it on your own. If you are helping someone else learn to manage his or her finances, you may find the guides in this series to be a helpful part of what you do together. Engaged and married couples also will find these guides invaluable when sorting out how to handle their finances jointly.

The following elements are included in the sessions.

*Approach Question(s)*. Most sessions begin with one or two questions that invite participants to share what they have been thinking and feeling about money during the week. These questions often refer to the homework assignment from the previous session. Group members have a chance to share what they have learned from the homework exercise.

*Teaching and Scripture*. Next there are several pages of teaching on a topic, built around a few key passages of Scripture. Ideally, participants should have read and digested this section before coming to the group meeting; but the text is brief enough to take ten minutes to read it during the meeting. Key paragraphs and Scripture passages could be reread during the meeting in order to discuss the questions.

*Discussion Questions*. These questions invite you to respond to the teaching and Scripture. Two people probably could cover them in twenty minutes; eight or ten people could use an hour, although forty minutes would be adequate. Some questions may provoke such a lively discussion that the leader will have to decide whether to cut off the discussion and move on or skip some of the later questions. When a question is personal, you always have the option of writing a full answer on your own and telling the group only what you feel is appropriate.

*The Grace Adventure*. Each session closes with a reminder that God's grace is available to accomplish what

His Word asks of us. God doesn't pile on a lot of commands and leave us to fend for ourselves.

This section also includes a suggestion about how to pray in response to what you have been discussing. Prayer is a way of acknowledging and seeking God's grace. If your group is accustomed to praying together, you may not need the suggestions to guide your prayers.

If some participants are unaccustomed to praying aloud, you may decide to make your prayer time brief, allow time for silent prayer only, or let some pray aloud and others remain silent. Decide on the ground rules for group prayer at your first meeting so that no one will fear being put on the spot later on.

*During the Week.* A Bible study guide typically asks you to study one or more Bible passages in preparation for your next group meeting. By contrast, this guide asks you to reflect on one or two of the verses you have just discussed. The idea is to let those key truths sink into your mind and heart.

You'll also be asked to pay attention to the way you handle money during the week in light of what you have been discussing. Meditating on Scripture and observing your own behavior work together to help you really listen to what God is telling you to do. Prayer will be a part of this listening.

Finally, you'll be asked to read the teaching for the next session. If you only have time to either read the next session or to do the other homework activities, choose the meditating and observing. However, reading ahead should take you only about ten minutes and will save a lot of time during your group meeting.

I trust that the Holy Spirit will guide you to examine your financial life through the teaching of God's Word.

\*    \*    \*    \*

*"Hold on to instruction, do not let it go; guard it well, for it is your life"* (Proverbs 4:13).

# FREELY YOU HAVE RECEIVED

When I advise struggling young couples to give 10 percent of their hard-earned incomes to God's work, many of them think I'm being amusingly idealistic. Some think it's only natural that pastors and others who live on the gifts of those they serve should teach tithing—it's in their best interest, after all. When I explain that the concept of giving comes directly from God, eyebrows tend to rise. God asks us to give primarily because giving is good for us. But the truth is, giving *is* good for us when we give for the right reasons. *"Honor the Lord from your wealth, and from the first of all your produce; so your barns will be filled with plenty, and your vats will overflow with new wine"* (Proverbs 3:9–10).

In this study, we will explore how the Bible answers several key questions:

What does it mean to tithe?
How much should I give?
Why should I give?
What should be my motivation?
What are bad reasons for giving, and why are they bad?
Does it matter who or what I give to?

First, take a moment to get to know the others in your

group. Money is a private subject, and for many of us the idea of discussing how much we give to whom and why is as appealing as discussing our weight, age, and income. You will never be asked in this study to reveal the details of your personal financial decisions, but you will be discussing a topic that sparks strong feelings, so it helps to know a little about other group members. Give everyone in the group a chance to answer question 1 briefly. Then go around the group again, letting everyone discuss the answers. Then go to question 2.

1. Tell your name (unless everyone knows it) and one thing you remember about your parents' giving habits (or lack of giving habits) when you were a child.

2. Why did you decide to join this discussion on giving? What do you hope to get out of it?

   ❏ My pastor is making me do this.

   ❏ My spouse is making me do this.

   ❏ The group is making me do this.

   ❏ I know I'm stingy and figure I'd better do something about it.

   ❏ I want some peace of mind about handling all the requests for money I receive.

   ❏ I've heard people talk about tithing, and I want to know what the Bible really says about it.

❏ I'm a disorganized giver; I need a plan.

❏ I've heard people say, "Give and you shall receive." Is that a gimmick, or does the Bible really say that?

❏ Other (explain)

## Friends and Finances

The whole thing was originally Sue's idea. Dan and Rachel, a couple new to her church and town, wanted to make friends. Sue thought they would mesh well with Kellie and Michael. The five of them had dinner together once—and then again six weeks later. The fourth time they gathered, Dan invited Rick and Sondra; the next time, Tara joined. After about six months the group decided to meet every other week, and before a year had passed they were meeting weekly. What had begun as a purely social connection sharpened into a close-knit group with a clear purpose. Each of them wanted to discern what God's will was for his or her life.

Several in the group were faithful Bible readers, and they developed a habit of bringing passages they didn't understand to the group for discussion. One evening, after dinner, Dan posed a question to the group. "Look at this," he said, "*Give, and it will be given to you; good measure, pressed down, shaken together, running over, they will pour into your lap. For by your standard of measure it will be measured to you in return* (Luke 6:38). What do you make

13

of that? Do you have to give in order to receive? That sounds pretty calculated."

Kellie, who had not grown up in the church, asked, "How much does God expect us to give to His work?"

"Ten percent," Sondra quickly responded. "That's called 'tithing.'"

"Is that 10 percent before or after taxes?" asked Kellie.

"Neither!" said Dan. "Either way an actual tithe would be too much for us. Wow! That would be thousands of dollars. We don't have that kind of surplus to play with. You're talking the equivalent of a new minivan every four years!"

Rachel rolled her eyes. "We spend more at McDonald's in a year than we give to the church."

Everyone in the group agreed that tithing seemed to be more of an ideal than a realistic practice. After all, Rick and Sondra were barely making ends meet. Rick was in his second year of law school; Sondra was working as a secretary, and money was tight. Huge financial debts, due to student loans and credit cards, loomed ahead. Tithing had become a distant memory. For Tara, a single mom, giving 10 percent would mean significant sacrifice. She asked, "Should tithing come before meeting basic needs?"

After some heated debate about what the Bible actually says on the subject, the group decided to do some Bible research on how much they should give. They were amazed at what they discovered. They learned that *tithe* is simply an Old English word for "a tenth." It translates Hebrew and Greek words that mean the same. Ancient peoples commonly gave a tenth of their incomes to their gods, so Abraham gave a tenth of his war booty to the priest-king Melchizedek (Genesis 14:17–20), and Jacob vowed to give God a tenth of his income if God protected him in exile (Genesis 28:20–22). Later, the Law of Moses required all Israelites to give a tenth of their harvests to God as a sign of gratitude (Deuteronomy 26:1–15).

The tithes supported the Levites and priests (the equivalent to pastors, missionaries, and other church staff) who taught God's Word and managed the worship services (Numbers 18:20–29). The tithes also aided poor Israelites and even needy Gentiles living in Israelite cities (Deuteronomy 14:28–29). Third, the tithes funded the people's worship celebrations. There may have been more than one tithe, part of which supported worship and another that supported the needy. People also gave offerings over and above the tithe. Some say that 23 percent may have been a typical level of giving.

3. How does the following passage describe the purposes of the tithe? Underline the purposes you observe.

*"You shall surely tithe all the produce from what you sow, which comes out of the field every year. And you shall eat in the presence of the Lord your God, at the place where He chooses to establish His name, the tithe of your grain, your new wine, your oil, and the first-born of your herd and your flock, in order that you may learn to fear the Lord your God always. And if the distance is so great for you that you are not able to bring the tithe, since the place where the Lord your God chooses to set His name is too far away from you when the Lord your God blesses you, then*

*you shall exchange it for money, and bind the money in your hand and go to the place which the Lord your God chooses. And you may spend the money for whatever your heart desires, for oxen, or sheep, or wine, or strong drink, or whatever your heart desires; and there you shall eat in the presence of the Lord your God and rejoice, you and your household. Also you shall not neglect the Levite who is in your town, for he has no portion or inheritance among you.*

*"At the end of every third year you shall bring out of all the tithe of your produce in that year, and shall deposit it in your town. And the Levite, because he has no portion or inheritance among you, and the alien, the orphan and the widow who are in your town, shall come and eat and be sat-isfied, in order that the Lord your God may bless you in all the work of your hand which you do"* (Deuteronomy 14:22–29).

4. Who would be modern equivalents of the Levites, the aliens, the fatherless, and the widows in our society?

_____

_____

_____

_____

The tithe was not established in order to support elab-orate temple worship and full-time ministers but as a physical, earthly demonstration of man's commitment to God. God understood that people tend to think their possessions are theirs because they earned them, so He established the tithe to test whether they really acknowledged Him as owner of all.

The prophet Malachi confronted the people about the sneaky ways they avoided acknowledging God as supreme.

"'A son honors his father, and a servant his master. Then if I am a father, where is My honor? And if I am a master, where is My respect?' says the Lord of hosts to you, O priests who despise My name. But you say, 'How have we despised Thy name?'

"You are presenting defiled food upon My altar. But you say, 'How have we defiled Thee?' In that you say, 'The table of the Lord is to be despised.'

"But when you present the blind for sacrifice, is it not evil? And when you present the lame and sick, is it not evil? Why not offer it to your governor? Would he be pleased with you? Or would he receive you kindly?" says the Lord of hosts (Malachi 1:6–8).

"'Will a man rob God? Yet you are robbing Me! But you say "How have we robbed Thee?" In tithes and offerings.

"'You are cursed with a curse, for you are robbing Me, the whole nation of you!

"'Bring the whole tithe into the storehouse, so that there may be food in My house, and test Me now in this,' says the Lord of hosts, 'if I will not open for you the windows of heaven and pour out for you a blessing until it overflows.

"'Then I will rebuke the devourer for you, so that it may not destroy the fruits of the ground; nor will your vine in the field cast its grapes,' says the Lord of hosts.

"'All the nations will call you blessed, for you shall be a delightful land,' says the Lord of hosts" (Malachi 3:8–12).

The people were suffering from poor harvests, weak leadership, and enemy attacks, but Malachi said all their problems could be traced to their disrespect for God, demonstrated by their failure to tithe. Instead of begrudging God His 10 percent, the people should have been thanking Him for generously giving them 90 percent!

5. What wrong attitudes did Malachi say the people had toward God?

_____

_____

_____

_____

6. How were they displaying those wrong attitudes?

_____

_____

_____

_____

7. Why do you think it robbed and dishonored God to offer Him leftovers or an incomplete tithe?

_____

_____

_____

8. How do people today display the wrong attitudes
   Malachi condemned?

Dan was impressed that the Old Testament tithe was
used for celebrating thanks to God and caring for the
needy, but he wasn't convinced these passages in
Deuteronomy and Malachi applied to him. "What about
the rest of the ceremonial law?" he asked the group. "We
don't still cut up sheep or offer bread every week." Tithing
seemed like a legalism to Dan, and Kellie's question about
"before or after taxes" proved it. After all, the Israelites
may have given 10 percent or 23 percent to the Levites,
but they weren't also paying 35 percent of their income to
the government, were they?

Actually, under Solomon and the kings that followed
him, heavy taxes oppressed the people and were one reason the nation split in two. When foreign empires took
over, taxes were worse—almost nobody in the time of
Jesus could survive paying both the religious tithes and
the taxes to Rome. In session 2, we'll look at how the
New Testament answers these questions.

9. a.  Think about the passages from Deuteronomy and Malachi. In what ways do these passages reflect the idea of giving out of *gratitude for receiving?*

_____

_____

_____

_____

    b.  In what ways do these passages reflect giving out of *awareness that one belongs to the community of God's people?*

_____

_____

_____

_____

10.  What do you think Deuteronomy and Malachi have to say to us today?

_____

_____

_____

_____

_____

## The Grace Adventure

Is tithing law or grace? Is tithing relevant to us today? Do we look at tithing as an obligation or as an opportunity? Surely, when the Israelites gathered with their religious teachers, the needy, and even their non-Jewish neighbors, to celebrate how God had blessed them, there was a spirit of grace in the air. Israel is the only nation we know of in the Middle East that had laws about caring for the poor and noncitizens. Take one minute of silence together to ask God how His words in Deuteronomy and Malachi are relevant to you as individuals and as a group.

## During the Week

- Post and meditate on Malachi 1:6 this week: "'A *son honors his father, and a servant his master. Then if I am a father, where is My honor? And If I am a master, where is My respect?' says the Lord of hosts to you.*" As you think about this verse, ask yourself how well you are showing honor and respect to the Lord through the actions of your life (including your finances). How can you grow in this area? As you read this verse, what thoughts and feelings arise in you?

# THE GRACE OF GIVING

1. How do you think your life would be different a year from now if you consistently gave a tenth of your income to God? How would this affect your lifestyle? How would it affect your inner life?

## The New Testament

Dan balked at the idea that the Old Testament law of tithing applied to him, so he was eager to see what the New Testament said about it. Sue reminded the group that the New Testament refers to tithing twice. In Matthew 23:23 (NIV), Jesus condemned the hypocrites who gave a tenth of even their garden herbs but *"neglected the more important matters of the law—justice, mercy and faithfulness. You should have practiced the latter, without neglecting the former."* Hebrews 7:1–10 mentions Abraham's gift of a tenth to Melchizedek as an example of Abraham recognizing that king's authority.

"Doesn't it seem," asked Rachel, "that the New Testament extends the idea of the tithe, rather than eliminates it?"

Sue agreed. When the apostle Paul talked about giving, he didn't set a percentage. Instead, he pointed to Christ's no-holds-barred self-sacrifice as the standard. "You're right," said Rachel. "Giving is more of an attitude than a requirement."

In 2 Corinthians, Paul urges the Corinthian Christians to join with those in Macedonia in sending aid to believers in Judea, where the economy was in recession.

*"Now, brethren, we wish to make known to you the grace of God which has been given in the churches of Macedonia, that in a great ordeal of affliction their abundance of joy and their deep poverty overflowed in the wealth of their liberality.*

*"For I testify that according to their ability, and beyond their ability they gave of their own accord, begging us with much entreaty for the favor of participation in the support of the saints, and this, not as we had expected, but they first gave themselves to the Lord and to us by the will of God"* (2 Corinthians 8:1–5).

*"I am not speaking this as a command, but as proving through the earnestness of others the sincerity of your love also. For you know the grace of our Lord Jesus Christ, that though He was rich, yet for your sake He became poor, that you through His poverty might become rich.*

*"And I give my opinion in this matter, for this is to your advantage, who were the first to begin a year ago not only to do this, but also to desire to do it. But now finish doing it also; that just as there was the readiness to desire it, so there may be also the completion of it by your ability. For if the readiness is present, it is acceptable according to what a man has, not according to what he does not have"* (2 Corinthians 8:8–12).

*"Now this I say, he who sows sparingly shall also reap sparingly; and he who sows bountifully shall also reap boun-*

*tifully. Let each one do just as he has purposed in his heart; not grudgingly or under compulsion; for God loves a cheerful giver.*

*"And God is able to make all grace abound to you, that always having all sufficiency in everything, you may have an abundance for every good deed"* (2 Corinthians 9:6–8).

2. What ground rules for deciding how much to give does Paul lay out in this passage? Underline the ground rules he sets, then summarize what you observe.

_____

_____

_____

_____

_____

3. What attitudes does he encourage the Corinthians to have as they give?

_____

_____

_____

_____

4. Does it surprise you that the Macedonians begged *"with much entreaty for the favor of participation in the support of the saints"*? Why or why not?

 

 

 

The Macedonians pleaded for the privilege to be partners with Paul and his other churches in this fundraising project, because they recognized it as the supreme sign that they were part of the same community or family with God's people in Corinth and Judea. Ethnic conflict threatened to divide Jewish from Gentile Christians, but generosity could heal that breach. The Macedonians were able to recognize that they were one community (one family) with the Judean Christians, even though they were of a different race, had different customs and language, lived thousands of miles away, and would probably never see each other.

5. How easy is it for you to feel and act like family with people of different races or people who live in distant countries? What helps you in that? What hinders you?

 

 

 

Paul went on to tell the Corinthians, *"Now He who supplies seed to the sower and bread for food, will supply and multiply your seed for sowing and increase the harvest of your righteousness; you will be enriched in everything for all liberality, which through us is producing thanksgiving to God"* (2 Corinthians 9:10–11).

6. What does Paul say about the relationship between giving and receiving in 2 Corinthians 9:10?

_____

_____

_____

_____

Finally, Paul said, *"For the ministry of this service is not only fully supplying the needs of the saints, but is also overflowing through many thanksgivings to God. Because of the proof given by this ministry they will glorify God for your obedience to your confession of the gospel of Christ, and for the liberality of your contribution to them and to all, while they also, by prayer on your behalf, yearn for you because of the surpassing grace of God in you. Thanks be to God for His indescribable gift!"* (2 Corinthians 9:12–15).

7. What results did Paul expect from the Corinthians' generosity?

_____

_____

8. From what you have read in Matthew and in 2 Corinthians, how do you think Jesus and Paul would answer Dan's and Rachel's questions: "Am I supposed to give 10 percent of my income to God's work?" "Is that 10 percent before or after taxes?"

9. What do you think Jesus and Paul would say to someone who feels he or she can't afford to give more than 3 percent or 4 percent to God?

10. The Macedonians considered giving to the needy
    a privilege. Why do you suppose most people don't
    consider it a privilege?

_____

_____

_____

_____

When people view one another as family, 10 percent or
even more seems a privilege, not a burden. Giving is God's
way of involving us in His redemptive work of caring for
the needy, teaching His Word, spreading the Gospel, and
gathering His people for worship. We can consider it an
honor to be God's partner. Because of the grace we have
received, we won't think, *How little can I get away with giving?* Instead, we will ask ourselves, *How much can I manage
to give?*

## The Grace Adventure

Paul said the Macedonians' eagerness to give was *"grace"*
from God (2 Corinthians 8:1). This grace in them was a
response to *"the grace of our Lord Jesus Christ, that though
He was rich, yet for your sake He became poor, that you
through His poverty might become rich"* (2 Corinthians 8:9).
Having graciously received, they graciously gave, not
under compulsion, but enthusiastically. Further, said Paul,
*"God is able to make all grace abound* [to those who give],
*that always having all sufficiency in everything, you may have
an abundance for every good deed"* (2 Corinthians 9:8).

11. Take a few moments to ask God to give you the Macedonians' grace of enthusiastic giving, so that you will grow in grace both as you give and as you receive.

## During the Week

- Choose a sentence from the verses in 2 Corinthians 8–9 that encourages you in the grace of giving. Copy it and place it where you will see it often—on your refrigerator, in your checkbook, on your car visor. Memorize the verse this week.

- Take time (with your spouse if you are married) this week to study your budget and ask yourself, "How much can I manage to give?" Pray about this until you feel confident that you are making a wise decision for your present circumstances. Think about nonmonetary as well as monetary gifts.

- In Deuteronomy 14, we read that the Old Testament tithe was gathered in a storehouse and distributed to the needy by the Levites, Israel's spiritual leaders. Ideally, a church could function as a storehouse, distributing tithes to its staff, the poor, missionaries, and so on. To the extent that your church isn't equipped to serve in a specific area of ministry, you might choose to give part of your offering directly to another organization that is "filling the gap." But remember that you can't sit under the teaching of a local church and not support it financially (1 Timothy 5:17–18).

- Pray this week about how much you should give,
  but also pray about possible areas of your church's
  ministry that need your help. Is there a ministry
  you could be involved in that helps to meet the
  needs of God's people?

\*    \*    \*    \*

"'Bring the whole tithe into the storehouse, so that there may
be food in My house, and test Me now in this,' says the Lord of
hosts, 'if I will not open for you the windows of heaven, and
pour out for you a blessing until it overflows'" (Malachi 3:10).

"And the Lord has today declared you to be His people, a
treasured possession, as He promised you, and that you should
keep all His commandments; and that He shall set you high
above all nations which He has made, for praise, fame, and
honor; and that you shall be a consecrated people to the Lord
your God, as He has spoken" (Deuteronomy 26:18–19).

# GIVING TO RECEIVE

1. Think of a recent time when you received an appeal to give money to an organization. What strategy did that group use to urge or invite you to give? How did the appeal make you feel?

## Ulterior Motives

Dan started the group's discussion on giving once again. Tossing down a stack of letters on the coffee table, he said, "This is another thing that bugs me about churches and giving. Do you know how many letters we get asking for money? How are we supposed to support our church and meet all of these other needs? How do we even know that these organizations are legitimate?"

"I know," agreed Tara. "A few years ago I gave a gift to an organization that helps feed poor children. Now I am on mailing lists for dozens of organizations. My money is tight. I can't afford to help all of these people."

"I know that supporting God's work is important, but the need can be overwhelming," said Dan. "What's hard is keeping the right attitude." Dan read to the group: "*He who is kind to the poor lends to the Lord, and he will reward him for what he has done*" (Proverbs 19:17 NIV). Then Dan said, "When we give to the poor, whether they are Christians or not, we are literally lending to God, and He has promised to make sure that the resources will continue to be there."

Tara thought about this. "I have a friend who likes to say, 'You can't outgive God.' She quotes where Jesus says, '*Give, and it will be given to you. A good measure, pressed down, shaken together and running over, will be poured into your lap. For with the measure you use, it will be measured to you*' (Luke 6:38 NIV). But that feels odd to me. It reminds me of Steve Martin in the movie, *Leap of Faith*; he plays a con artist pretending to be an evangelist and faith healer. Martin keeps telling these hardworking farm people that if they give him money, then God will give them rain for their crops, heal their arthritis, and make them prosper financially. I don't know whether he's appealing to their fear that God won't bless them if they don't give, or to their greed, but either way it bothers me."

2. How could Luke 6:38 be used to appeal to someone's greed?

_____

_____

_____

3. How could it be used to appeal to someone's fear?

_____

_____

_____

4. What is wrong with appealing to people's guilt,
   greed, or fear when you are raising money for a good
   cause like evangelism or caring for the needy?

_____

_____

_____

The following is the story of a man named Simon who
wanted to give to the apostles in order to receive something from God.

"Now when the apostles in Jerusalem heard that Samaria
had received the word of God, they sent them Peter and
John, who came down and prayed for them, that they might
receive the Holy Spirit. For He had not yet fallen upon any
of them; they had simply been baptized in the name of the
Lord Jesus. Then they began laying their hands on them,
and they were receiving the Holy Spirit.

"Now when Simon saw that the Spirit was bestowed
through the laying on of the apostles' hands, he offered them
money, saying, 'Give this authority to me as well, so that
everyone on whom I lay my hands may receive the Holy
Spirit.'

"But Peter said to him, 'May your silver perish with you,
because you thought you could obtain the gift of God with
money! You have no part or portion in this matter, for your
heart is not right before God. Therefore repent of this
wickedness of yours, and pray the Lord that if possible, the

*intention of your heart may be forgiven you. For I see that you are in the gall of bitterness and in the bondage of iniquity"* (Acts 8:14–23).

5. What did Simon want from God?

6. Why do you think he wanted it?

7. What was wrong with Simon giving in order to receive from God?

When we give in order to bribe God into blessing us, we do not receive that blessing. People who pull verses out of context and wave them in God's face as a demand are generally disappointed. We are to give primarily in order to express our gratitude for all we have received from God and our awareness that we are neighbors to the needy, to citizens of the kingdom, and to partners in the Gospel. Giving that does not grow out of grateful awareness of *koinonia,* of belonging to the community of God, will falter.

## A Friend in Need

One evening, Sue received a phone call. "Sue, you can't believe what's happened," said Kellie. She sounded upset.

"What's wrong, Kellie?" asked Sue.

"It's Michael's job," said Kellie. "His company has been bought out by a bigger corporation. They're reducing the sales staff by half. Michael didn't want to tell me when he first got home, but since he was so quiet, I knew something was wrong."

"Will he lose his job?" asked Sue.

"They gave him one week to decide." said Kellie. "He either can take two months' severance pay or we'll have to relocate to Atlanta. If we relocate, he starts at his new job a week from Monday."

"Wow. How are *you* doing?" asked Sue.

"I'm okay," said Kellie. "We're both just stunned. I guess we don't have much of a choice."

During the next few weeks, the group's focus shifted to helping Kellie and Michael. They all pitched in to help Kellie pack and get the house ready to sell. Dan and Rick went to breakfast with Michael and prayed with him about the move. Much to Kellie's surprise, the house sold quickly.

While Michael looked for a place in Atlanta and Kellie finished her last month and a half of teaching school, Sue insisted that Kellie move into her home. Sue was a wonderful friend during those next weeks. She listened when Kellie spoke of her loneliness.

Kellie and Michael were about to see God's hand in this major change in their lives.

What does this have to do with giving? After all, no money changed hands. Nonetheless, this experience set Kellie's understanding of giving for the rest of her life. Why? Because it gave her a first taste of the kind of community the Bible calls *koinonia* (fellowship, sharing, participation) and "the kingdom of God." It taught her what Jesus meant when He sent His followers into the world with the mandate, *"Freely you received, freely give"* (Matthew 10:8).

Until the night she phoned Sue, Kellie had been moderately grateful for God's gift of eternal life, but freely receiving that gift had not made her an enthusiastically generous person. To tell the truth, she took salvation for granted. She had even taken their financial security for granted.

She was moderately grateful for her middle-class lifestyle, but deep down she thought the possessions she had accumulated through her job, her parents, and her marriage to Michael were hers—she or those close to her had earned them. But when Sue took her in and when the rest of the group cared for her and Michael during the long, tense process of his layoff and their move, Kellie felt saved—rescued, championed, welcomed, healed—really for the first time.

Because faith is a personal decision and America is an individualistic country, many people act as if the Christian life is a one-to-one, hermit-like relationship with God. But as Kellie and Michael discovered, following Christ involves being born into a family, becoming a citizen of a kingdom (the word *Christ* means "anointed King").

Giving and receiving is the lifeblood of the community's relationship with God—receiving mercy and giving praise—and it is also the lifeblood of relationships among the family. Community members don't give because some bylaw requires them to do so; they begin to give freely when they begin to receive freely and recognize how much they have received.

8. What did Kellie and Michael receive from the community of believers during crisis?

_____

_____

_____

_____

_____

9. What do you think Kellie and Michael received from God during this process?

_____

_____

_____

_____

10. Have you ever experienced this kind of care from God's people? If so, tell about your experience and how it affected you. If not, what has been your

experience of receiving, or not receiving, from God's people?

_____

_____

_____

_____

_____

_____

11. Why do you suppose receiving forgiveness, peace with God, and eternal life doesn't motivate all Christians to be generous?

_____

_____

_____

_____

The Gospels sum up Jesus' message with a phrase: "*Repent, for the kingdom of heaven* [or God] *is at hand*" (Matthew 4:17). Also see Mark 1:15. "*The kingdom of heaven*" was a Jewish term for the realm where God ruled with justice and with what we might call "wholeness." The Greek word *soteria* is translated at various times as "salvation" or "healing." The Hebrew word *shalom* could be translated as "wholeness," "prosperity," "well-being," or "peace." The citizens of the kingdom would be whole in body, mind, and spirit; their relationships with each other and with God would be whole; even death would be forgotten. When Jesus arrived, the kingdom was near because the King was near.

Jesus chose twelve disciples to experience kingdom life intensively. It can't have been easy, since they came from conflicting social backgrounds and political leanings, but they were forced to learn to care for one another. Having left their jobs and families to follow Jesus, they were obliged to live on charity from the ones Jesus healed and taught. When Jesus finally sent them out to do what He had been doing for months, He told them, *"As you go, preach this message: 'The kingdom of heaven is near.' Heal the sick, raise the dead, cleanse those who have leprosy, drive out demons. Freely you have received, freely give"* (Matthew 10:7–8 NIV).

12. What had the disciples freely received from God?

13. What have you freely received from God?

## The Grace Adventure

In the Bible, *grace* refers to two generous gifts God gives us. One is the welcoming forgiveness He offers us when we fall far short of His standard for a wise and loving life. The other is the empowering presence of the Holy Spirit within us—the Spirit who can enable us to become people we never dreamed of being. Unless we believe firmly that God extends grace to us with both hands, we likely will find that studying His principles about giving will produce little but guilt and rationalization. But if we believe in grace, then these same principles can become doorways to an adventure in living by grace.

14. If your group is large, divide into groups of two or three. Tell your partners one thing this session prompts you to ask God for. Then, either in silence together or aloud, ask God to do those things for your partners.

## During the Week

- Sometime this week, take half an hour to think about your past history of receiving. Get some paper and a pen. Divide your life into decades, and write whatever you remember receiving from your earliest days until age nine, from ages ten to nineteen, and so on. You might recall specific stories and/or a general state of affairs. Include material, emotional, intellectual, and spiritual things you received. Also write what you remember not receiving that you needed or wanted.

Then sit back and read over what you've written. Do you see a person who feels well provided for or one who has been deprived at various stages of his or her life? How do you feel as you read this?

• Also, copy onto a card or sheet of notepaper the sentence, *"Freely you received, freely give"* (Matthew 10:8). Post it where you will see it often during the week. Each time you see it, read it, and think about what it is saying to you. Take note of how it makes you feel: uncomfortable? convicted? encouraged? grateful? Think about what you have freely received from God and/or His people during the past twenty-four hours.

# FREELY GIVE

1. Tell the group one thing you learned about yourself from reviewing your history of receiving. (If you didn't get a chance to write out a whole history, tell the group one thing you remember receiving as a child and one thing you remember not receiving.)

## The Shared Life

As Kellie felt her life getting back in order, she began to think less about what she needed from her group and more about what she could give back to them. She and Michael insisted that Kellie would help Sue by paying half of the rent and utilities, and she looked for other ways she could help Sue. She talked less about herself in the group and asked more questions about what others were going through.

When Sondra had a difficult last few weeks of pregnancy, Kellie took her turn at cooking for Sondra's family, as well as helping to organize her shower.

Kellie and Michael phoned each other frequently and commited to pray each day for one another and for the needs of their friends. Kellie's prayer life had received a boost from her experience of receiving God's love from her friends. She thanked God for Sue and the others in the group almost every day.

Kellie also began to think about increasing their financial contribution to the church. She had learned a lot about the Bible from her pastor's teaching, and he had welcomed her and Michael as newcomers to the church.

What the apostle Paul said seemed to apply to her: *"Anyone who receives instruction in the word must share all good things with his instructor"* (Galatians 6:6 NIV).

Jesus told His disciples to expect that those who received ministry would support the ministers *"for the worker is worthy of his support"* (Matthew 10:10).

Although Kellie had been trying to tithe to the church, she realized now how much she had benefited from the worship and teaching her church provided; and she was convinced she should help to pay for those things. She had received freely; there was no requirement to pay for the ministry she had received. However, having received freely, she began to want to give back freely.

When we first begin to sense the Holy Spirit prompting us to give, sometimes in a way that extends beyond our tithe, we usually think first of those from whom we have received. We become alert to their needs and think, *What is my part in meeting this need?* We ask God. Sometimes we are prompted to contribute money, as Kellie was prompted to give to her church. Sometimes we can offer our time and labor, as Kellie did when she cooked for Sondra's family. Sometimes people need our listening, caring ears. Sometimes the richest gift we can offer is prayer.

Jesus said, *"Love each other as I have loved you. Greater love has no one than this, that he lay down his life for his friends"* (John 15:12–13 NIV). Kellie's first steps in giving as she had received involved learning how to love those in her immediate family of believers—her close friends. These were significant steps. Many people never learn

how to love even those closest to them. But while receiving gave her a first taste of biblical community, sharing in
the community's labor drew her deeper in.

*Koinonia* is a key New Testament concept. A form of
this word is translated "share" in Galatians 6:6. The apostle Paul used the same word to describe the way the
Philippians acted as partners with him in his work by supporting him financially. *"Always offering prayer with joy in
my every prayer for you all, in view of your participation in
the gospel from the first day until now. . . . For it is only right
for me to feel this way about you all, because I have you in my
heart, since both in my imprisonment and in the defense and
confirmation of the gospel, you all are partakers of grace with
me* (Philippians 1:4–5,7; compare 4:14–15). *Koinonia* is
also often translated as "fellowship": *"They were continual-
ly devoting themselves to the apostles' teaching and to **fellowship**, to the breaking of bread and to prayer"* (Acts 2:42,
emphasis added).

*Koinonia* is the sharing of lives and mission that char-
acterizes true biblical community. It grows out of the joint
experience of sharing Christ's grace and suffering and our
common hope of sharing His glory (Romans 8:17; Philippians 1:7, 3:10).

Kellie began to have fellowship with her friends and
her church when she received ministry from them. She
was drawn deeper into fellowship when she gave back to
them and shared the job of caring for the members of her
group and her church. Giving was a natural outgrowth of
her sense of partnership with them in the Gospel.

2. What did Kellie give to her group and her church at
　　this stage of her growth?

_____

_____

_____

_____

3. How do you think giving in these ways helped Kellie
   to grow?

_____

_____

_____

_____

4. Can you identify with Kellie in any ways? How is
   your experience like or unlike hers?

_____

_____

_____

_____

_____

5. In what specific ways do you benefit from the
   ministries of your church? Make a list.

_____

6.  In what ways do you receive from this group or other groups to which you belong?

7.  What needs are you aware of

    in your church?

    in this group or other groups you belong to?

8. Select one or more of those needs and discuss how you as individuals or as a group might respond to that need through money, time, skills, and/or prayer.

## The Grace Adventure

We are not necessarily responsible for meeting every need we see. It's important to ask God to enable us to discern those needs to which we should respond. We also should ask Him *how* He wants us to respond.

9. Take five minutes to pray about the needs you mentioned in question 7 and the ideas you thought of in question 8. Ask God to impress on each participant's heart the needs he or she should respond to, along with the response He desires.

## During the Week

• Copy one of the following verses onto a card, and post it with Matthew 10:8.

   *"Always offering prayer with joy in my every prayer*

*for you all, in view of your participation in the gospel from the first day until now"* (Philippians 1:4–5).

*"Anyone who receives instruction in the word must share all good things with his instructor"* (Galatians 6:6 NIV).

*"Love each other as I have loved you. Greater love has no one than this, that he lay down his life for his friends"* (John 15:12–13 NIV).

• In the last session you assessed your history of receiving; this time set aside half an hour to think about your history of *giving*. Your history includes giving to the church, other charities, and even individuals who have needed something. This includes your tithes, other financial gifts, and your contributions of time and resources. Get some paper and a pen. Divide your life into decades, and write whatever you remember about giving or not giving—from your earliest days to age nine, from ages ten to nineteen, and so on. You might recall specific stories, habits, or maybe nothing; if the latter is the case, write "nothing." Then read over what you've written. Do you see a person who has been habitually generous? overly generous in some cases? fairly stingy, all things considered? How do you feel about what you see?

# WIDENING THE CIRCLE

1. Tell the group about a time when you enjoyed giving a gift to someone.

## Comfort

After spending so much time with Kellie and Michael and helping them deal with the problems they had faced, Sue decided she wanted to be a small group leader in her church's counseling support groups. She never had been the type who volunteered for a dozen committees in order to feel worthwhile; nor did she feel compulsively driven to stay busy. She simply read Paul's words: *"Praise be to the God and Father of our Lord Jesus Christ, the Father of compassion and the God of all comfort, who comforts us in all our troubles, so that we can comfort those in any trouble with the comfort we ourselves have received from God"* (2 Corinthians 1:3–4 NIV).

As a busy mother of two, Sue was well equipped to serve the emotional needs of the group members assigned to her. She could listen to people express their anger, sadness, and confusion without rushing to make them feel better. She could show that there was light at the end of the tunnel. She could care. But some of the members' more material needs stirred up surprising emotions in her.

Denise, one of the newest group members, was barely making ends meet as a single mother of three. As December arrived, she talked about how frustrated and ashamed she felt because she had absolutely no money for Christmas. The group took a break for the holidays, but Sue continued to see Denise at church. One Sunday, a tearful Denise described to Sue the porcelain doll her eleven-year-old wanted and how it symbolized all the ways she had cried when her five-year-old asked why they didn't have anything under their Christmas tree, Sue decided she had to do something.

She went to the mall and found the store with the porcelain dolls Denise described. Surveying the display, she asked herself, "Why am I doing this?" In part she was indulging the little girl part of herself, who would still like to have dolls if she weren't too grown up for all that. Another part of her thought of her own daughter, whose eyes would light up at the sight of a new doll. Giving seemed like a positive way to handle those feelings. So Sue had a great time buying and wrapping the doll, as well as gifts for Denise's other two children.

Her first impulse was to leave the gifts on Denise's doorstep anonymously because Jesus said, "*Be careful not to do your 'acts of righteousness' before men, to be seen by them. If you do, you will have no reward from your Father in heaven. So when you give to the needy, do not announce it with trumpets, as the hypocrites do in the synagogues and on the streets, to be honored by men. I tell you the truth, they have received their reward in full. But when you give to the needy, do not let your left hand know what your right hand is doing, so that your giving may be in secret. Then your Father, who sees what is done in secret, will reward you*" (Matthew 6:1–4 NIV).

After praying about it, Sue decided that it would embarrass Denise not to know whom to thank. She knew that Jesus probably was more concerned that she did *not* announce to the rest of the church what she was doing.

2. Why was Sue motivated to volunteer for the support group?

_____

_____

_____

_____

3. In what ways does her desire to help reflect her understanding of giving?

_____

_____

_____

_____

4. What do you think of Sue's decision to buy gifts for Denise's children? What would you have done in Sue's place?

_____

_____

_____

_____

_____

5. a. Look at what Jesus says about the hypocrites in Matthew 6:1–4. What is wrong with their motive for giving?

_____

_____

b. Do you agree or disagree with Sue's decision not to leave the gifts anonymously? Why?

_____

_____

_____

_____

Her experiences with the support group made Sue think her church needed a much more organized way of caring for the materially needy among them. Both had long-term, as well as short-term, needs for financial counsel and assistance. The terms "poor" and "needy" began to leap off the pages of her Bible at her every day.

_It seems that God is constantly urging His people to care as much for the needy as He does_, she thought.

6. The following is a sample of the many biblical references to the poor and needy. How do you think each of these is relevant today?

> _"If one of your countrymen becomes poor and is unable to support himself among you, help him as you would an alien or a temporary resident, so he can continue to live among you"_ (Leviticus 25:35 NIV).

56

"For the Lord your God is the God of gods and the Lord of lords, the great, the mighty, and the awesome God who does not show partiality, nor take a bribe. He executes justice for the orphan and the widow, and shows His love for the alien by giving him food and clothing. So show your love for the alien, for you were aliens in the land of Egypt" (Deuteronomy 10:17–19).

"If there is a poor man with you, one of your brothers, in any of your towns in your land which the Lord your God is giving you, you shall not harden your heart, nor close your hand from your poor brother; but you shall freely open your hand to him, and shall generously lend him sufficient for his need in whatever he lacks. Beware, lest there is a base thought in your heart, saying, 'The seventh year, the year of remission, is near,' and your eye is hostile toward your poor brother, and you give him nothing; then he may cry to the Lord against you, and it will be a sin in you. You shall generously give to him, and your *heart shall not be grieved when you give to him, because for this thing the Lord your God will bless you in all your work and in all your undertakings. For the poor will never cease to be in the land; therefore I command you, saying, 'You shall freely open your hand to your brother, to your needy and poor in your land'"* (Deuteronomy 15:7–11).

*"Is this not the fast which I choose, to loosen the bonds of wickedness, to undo the bands of the yoke, and to let the oppressed go free, and break every yoke? Is it not to divide your bread with the hungry, and bring the homeless poor into the house; when you see the naked, to cover him; and not to hide yourself from your own flesh? Then your light will break out like the dawn, and your recovery will speedily spring forth; and your righteousness will go before you; the glory of the Lord will be your rear guard. Then you will call, and the Lord will answer; you will cry, and He will say, 'Here I am'"* (Isaiah 58:6–9).

*"Behold, this was the guilt of your sister Sodom: she and her daughters had arrogance, abundant food, and careless ease, but she did not help the poor and needy"* (Ezekiel 16:49).

*"This is pure and undefiled religion in the sight of our God and Father, to visit orphans and widows in their distress, and to keep oneself unstained by the world"* (James 1:27).

*"But whoever has the world's goods, and beholds his brother in need and closes his heart against him, how does the love of God abide in him?"* (1 John 3:17).

7. Who in our culture would qualify as "widows," "orphans," and "the poor and needy"?

8. What emotions do you feel when reading these passages about the needy?

When Sue started coming to grips with the great needs around her and the consistent message in God's Word about the needy, she felt overwhelmed. But by praying consistently, she was able to regulate her emotions—confusion, sadness, anger, guilt that she wasn't doing enough—enough to listen to God for some direction.

## The Grace Adventure

When we feel guilty for not doing for the poor what the Bible says and also feel helpless to do what it says, we're likely to resolve our frustration by ignoring both. But God offers forgiveness for our failings, wisdom to devise an effective strategy, and strength to follow through. Alone, we can do little for the world's poor; together, we can do a lot.

9. Divide into groups of three. As you pray, tell God what you feel when you think about caring for the needy. Ask Him whatever questions come to mind when you think about this subject. Pray for the people you know who are struggling emotionally or financially.

## During the Week

• Post 1 John 3:17 this week, and think about what it means in your life.

• Be alert this week to all the ways you receive information about and appeals for the needy. Do you get letters in the mail asking you for money? Do television news stories depict the poor in foreign countries or describe a political debate about government welfare in this country? Do you see poor or homeless people on the streets as you go through your day? Take note of how these experiences affect you. What do you feel? How do you respond?

# GETTING ORGANIZED

1. Calculate how much money and other gifts you have given to God in the past year. How does that make you feel? Are you surprised at how much or how little you gave? Are you pleased? Disappointed? Proud? Embarrassed?

## The Hope Fund

Sue's pastor had invited her to be a part of a new church ministry fund, the Hope Fund. Rachel decided to attend the first meeting with Sue.

Their pastor, Pastor Mike, opened the meeting: "Our Lord said, *'By this all men will know that you are My disciples, if you have love for one another.'* That's John 13:35. One of the most important ways we can attract outsiders to Christ is by showing the kind of love for each other that can only be supernatural. But often, supernatural love is very practical. James 2:14–17 says, *'What use is it, my brethren, if a man says he has faith, but he has no works? Can that faith save him? If a brother or sister is without clothing and in need of daily food, and one of you says to them, "Go in peace, be warmed and be filled," and yet you do not give them what is necessary for their body, what use is that? Even so faith, if it has no works, is dead, being by itself.'* That kind of 'faith' is dead because it isn't faith in the real God. The real God is the head of a family in which His children have responsibilities toward one another.

"All of you know that our church is full of people who need practical help. In the past our church has been wary of benevolence funds because so often they are mismanaged. Several of us have been thinking about this, and we have a strategy that we believe will target real needs, screen out anyone who just wants to take advantage, and give the kind of help that doesn't demean people but helps them get on their feet.

"Many people think we shouldn't have to have a 'welfare' program in the church because we already pay a lot of taxes to support government welfare. My thought is that government got into the welfare business only because the church wasn't doing its job, and the government can't do what people really need: love them as individuals, tailor help to their unique needs, help them keep a budget, and encourage them when things are tough."

The pastor's plan included having applicants fill out a questionnaire and then sit down with an interviewer to write out a current budget. Since many people have no idea what they are actually spending on what, the interviewers needed to be trained to walk a person through a budget and watch for red flags. Interviewers also needed training to be both discerning and compassionate, knowing that the people who most need help often feel ashamed of their situation. Pastor Mike planned to preach on compassion during the upcoming stewardship drive, but the theme would have to be repeated over and over throughout the ministries of the church in order for people to get the message: Having needs doesn't make people second-class.

The Hope Fund Committee would use the application to assess a person's needs. Food, clothing, shelter (including utilities), and access to work (such as car repairs) would take priority. Money would be given only in rare exceptions. As a rule, the committee would prefer to pay the rent or utility bill or buy the food. The committee would decide whether a person needed short-term or long-term help. If a short-term, no-interest loan would solve the problem, the committee would lend the money.

Every individual or couple receiving financial aid would be required to have both spiritual and financial counseling. A lay financial counselor would meet monthly with them to be sure their budgets were working and to give encouragement. Most households can get by on their earnings if they learn to manage them skillfully. A lay pastoral counselor would meet with the individual or couple to explore the spiritual needs underlying their financial troubles. Support groups for those in financial difficulty also would be available.

"We will stress that needing counseling is not something to be ashamed of," Pastor Mike said. "The fact is that losing a job or making a financial mistake often puts stress on relationships between husbands and wives and between an individual and God, and we want to help people weather those storms. Also, money troubles are often rooted in spiritual issues like fear or pride, and the Bible urges us to address the roots of problems, not just the symptoms. We'll train the counselors not to be judgmental or coercive. We want them always to ask themselves, 'What would I be willing to do if I were in this person's shoes?'"

The Hope Fund program would require three things from the congregation: money, other resources, and volunteers. "Money" was obvious; "other resources" would include food, clothes, and a network of information on available jobs. Pastor Mike also hoped to find volunteers to donate their professional services to one or two households, such as medical care, dental care, legal help, and auto repair. He asked those gathered at the meeting if they would lead the effort to find volunteers to be trained as interviewers, lay counselors, and Hope Fund Committee members. Sue and Rachel were glad to sign up.

2. Why do you suppose Jesus said practical love for one another would be one of His people's most effective evangelism tools?

3. What did James say in James 2:14–17 about the faith of a church that doesn't care for its members' physical needs? Why would he say that?

4. If care for one another is so essential, why doesn't every church have a program like the Hope Fund program?

5. a.   What do you like about the Hope Fund program?

   b.   Is there anything that troubles you about it? If so, what?

6. What has to happen in the hearts of its people in order for a church to have an effective ministry to the needy?

7. Do you think churches need to organize programs
   like these, or do you think individual members or the
   church leadership should care for people in need?
   Explain your view.

_____

_____

_____

_____

_____

8. Why do many people believe that having needs is
   something to be ashamed of, even though the Bible
   says, *"For the poor will never cease to be in the land;
   therefore I command you, saying, 'You shall freely open
   your hand to your brother, to your needy and poor in
   your land'"* ( Deuteronomy 15:11).

_____

_____

_____

_____

9. How can a church, or other community of believers,
   communicate the message that having needs isn't
   something to be ashamed of?

_____

_____

Sue was happy to help with the Hope Fund program, but she had several concerns. As she and Rachel drove home, they talked about what Scripture meant when it said we are to care for our "brothers." They also talked about what was meant by the other *"needy and poor in your land."* In the story of the Good Samaritan (Luke 10:25–37), Jesus taught His followers to respond to needs of insiders and outsiders alike. The way Jesus defined a "neighbor," even people on the other side of the world would be included and, certainly, the poor on the other side of town.

Sue had another concern. Taking care of just their own members, let alone the rest of the city and the world, was going to take a lot of money. She thought that the whole issue of money was connected to her trust in God. Could she trust God to provide for her needs and for the needs of others?

Rachel asked Sue why she would give to the Hope Fund. She thought for a moment, then told her about how loved Kellie and Michael felt when the group had cared for them when they faced their problems. She said she believed that people in their town would be drawn to investigate Christ because their church was generous to its neighbors. She said knowing that God would reward her might give her the courage to be generous even on her tight budget.

10. Think about non-Christians who live across town from you and whom you don't know personally. How easy is it for you to care about them as neighbors? What helps you care about them in that way? What hinders you?

 

 

 

 

 

## The Grace Adventure

11. As you think about the physical needs of those in your church or community, what are you prompted to ask God? Take some time to voice to God your questions, concerns, doubts, and hopes about caring for His people.

## During the Week

- Post James 2:14–16: "*What use is it, my brethren, if a man says he has faith, but he has no works? Can that faith save him? If a brother or sister is without clothing and in need of daily food, and one of you says to them, 'Go in peace, be warmed and be filled,' and yet you do not give them what is necessary for their body, what use is that?*" Set aside some time this week to think and pray about what your part might be in caring for the needs of God's people.

# COURAGEOUS GIVING

1. How much do you equate money with feeling safe? List the top five things that make your life feel secure. What role does money play on that list? Is your financial situation an important source of security? of insecurity? Should it be?

## Protecting Our Treasures

Tara had an interesting question to pose to the group. As a single mom, she was concerned about her own future and her daughters. As hard as she worked, it was hard to keep up with bills, let alone plan for her future and give to others. Late at night, she often found herself staying awake worrying about how she would make ends meet. She was afraid that money was becoming too great of a focus in her life. What she had learned in her group meetings had impressed on her that she should start giving to her church. She wondered, *What should be my priority? Should I be giving money to the church when I am not able to start saving money?*

Dan agreed. "With all of this talk about giving God a tenth of my money, I get worried about how we should be spending our money. Is it right to save for a bigger home or a nicer car? Rachel and I really want to do what is right, but is it also right to use our money to please ourselves and our children? To be perfectly honest, it seems like we struggle between what we *want* to do with our money and what we *should* do."

"I agree," said Rick. "You know how Sondra and I are scraping by until I can finish school. Like Tara, we worry about how to pay bills. It is hard not to be a bit envious of others who don't have the same problems we do."

The group began to discuss what their attitudes should be toward money. Each situation was different. Dan and Rachel had two incomes but also two growing children. Rick and Sondra were on a limited budget while he was finishing law school. They owed a lot of money to student loans. Tara, a single mom, felt stretched to even meet basic needs.

Searching through Scripture to see how God wanted them to view their money, the group stumbled on some interesting passages. What better place was there to begin than with the wisdom of Proverbs:

> "Two things I asked of Thee, do not refuse me before I die: keep deception and lies far from me, give me neither poverty nor riches; feed me with the food that is my portion, lest I be full and deny Thee and say, 'Who is the Lord?' Or lest I be in want and steal, and profane the name of my God" (Proverbs 30:7–9).

The speaker in this proverb is identified as Agur (meaning "gatherer"). Although some disagree, many scholars have identified Agur as King Solomon. Regardless, his point about our attitudes toward money is a good one. The key to having a healthy, godlike attitude toward money is balance.

2. The author asks for two things: to keep deception and lies from him and to be neither rich nor poor. How do these two goals connect? Why are they equally important?

_____

_____

_____

_____

3. Why does having too much or too little distract us from God and His will for our lives?

_____

_____

_____

_____

The key to balancing our relationship with money seems to lie in our attitudes. When we have too little money, the human response is to worry and fear for our future. When we have too much, we tend to forget God and to rely on our own abilities to survive.

God's main concern for each of us is our attitudes. In God's Word, the apostle Paul tells us how to maintain the right perspective toward life, faith, and money.

*"Be anxious for nothing, but in everything by prayer and supplication with thanksgiving let your requests be made known to God. And the peace of God, which surpasses all comprehension, shall guard your hearts and your minds in Christ Jesus.*

*"Finally, brethren, whatever is true, whatever is honorable, whatever is right, whatever is pure, whatever is lovely, whatever is of good repute, if there is any excellence and if anything worthy of praise, let your mind dwell on these things. The things you have learned and received and heard and seen in me, practice these things, and the God of peace shall be with you.*

*"But I rejoiced in the Lord greatly, that now at last you have revived your concern for me; indeed, you were concerned before, but you lacked opportunity. Not that I speak from want; for I have learned to be content in whatever circumstances I am. I know how to get along with humble means, and I also know how to live in prosperity; in any and every circumstance I have learned the secret of being filled and going hungry, both of having abundance and suffering need. I can do all things through Him who strengthens me"* (Philippians 4:6–13).

Paul is speaking of the contrast between his external circumstances and his inner contentment. How can we be calm and trusting when the bills keep appearing and money is tight?

4. What does Paul mean when he says *"be anxious for nothing"*? Is that an easy attitude to maintain?

5. List things that Paul tells us to *"dwell on"* in verse 8.
   How does focusing on these things help us in times of
   trouble?

6. Specifically, what is Paul speaking about when he
   said he had learned to be content in an circumstance?

7. Why do people today have trouble with contentment? What things keep us from being content?

Paul says, *"I have learned the secret of being filled and going hungry, both of having abundance and suffering need"*(Philippians 4:12). The apostle was speaking from his own experience. Whether locked in a prison cell or staying with friends, he had learned to be content, to trust in God for his strength. He had learned that the key to contentment, the key to survival, was placing His trust in God. *"I can do all things through Him who strengthens me"* (Philippians 4:13).

Yet, the apostle was also speaking to the Philippians about sacrifice. They were to take this opportunity to help him with a gift. He was in need, and he knew that he could count on these fellow believers to meet that need.

"Yes," said Kellie. "When Michael and I were first faced with his possible layoff, we didn't have time to focus on how God would provide for our financial needs. But each of you took the time to meet those needs. Sue let me stay with her, and each of you helped by praying and listening. Money wasn't really the issue, but you took the time to meet our need. That whole experience has changed our attitudes about giving. Michael and I will never forget how you've helped us."

Sondra said that one passage that had really helped her and Rick maintain a positive attitude during the past few years was Jesus' words in Matthew 6:24–34, in which Jesus tells us not to worry about the lack of money. He issues the following caution.

"No one can serve two masters; for either he will hate the one and love the other, or he will hold to one and despise the other. You cannot serve God and mammon.

"For this reason I say to you, do not be anxious for your life, as to what you shall eat, or what you shall drink; nor for your body, as to what you shall put on. Is not life more than food, and the body than clothing? Look at the birds of the air, that they do not sow, neither do they reap, nor gather into barns, and yet your heavenly Father feeds them. Are you not worth much more than they? And which of you by being anxious can add a single cubit to his life's span?

"And why are you anxious about clothing? Observe how the lilies of the field grow; they do not toil nor do they spin, yet I say to you that even Solomon in all his glory did not clothe himself like one of these. But if God so arrays the grass of the field, which is alive today and tomorrow is thrown into the furnace, will He not much more do so for you, O men of little faith?

"Do not be anxious then, saying, 'What shall we eat?' or" 'What shall we drink?' or 'With what shall we clothe ourselves?' For all these things the Gentiles eagerly seek; for your heavenly Father knows that you need all these things. But seek first His kingdom and His righteousness; and all these things shall be added to you. Therefore do not be anxious for tomorrow; for tomorrow will care for itself. Each day has enough trouble of its own" (Matthew 6:24–34).

8. Underline the number of times Jesus speaks of being anxious (which means to worry). What are we not to worry about? Why?

9. What does it mean to serve money? When we turn our back on concerns about money and strive instead to serve God, what will be the result?

Remember that the people Jesus was speaking to did not frequent shopping malls; they did not visit mega-super-markets. These were farmers and peasants who owned no more than two, and probably only one, change of clothing. Each day's wage paid for that day's food. There were no credit cards and no money market funds, just the daily pressures of survival. In many ways, His audience had the right to be anxious. Yet, He told them, *Do not worry.*

10. Do you worry about money? How do Jesus' words correct your way of thinking?

_____

_____

_____

Our attitudes toward our own circumstances and our finances can greatly affect the way we feel about giving. If we tend to worry about money, we also will tend to hold tightly to what we have. We may justify not giving to God's work because we feel that our own needs will not be met. On the other hand, if our focus on money and things increases our success, we face the danger of forgetting God and neglecting His will for our lives. Money can become an all-consuming focus. We may skip Sunday services because we need to handle a few problems at work. We may lose interest in our families and our fellowship with believers. It is easy for money to turn our heads away from the things of God.

"No one can serve two masters." Whether we have been blessed with a great deal of money or struggle because we do not have enough, Jesus tells us to *"Seek first God's kingdom."* Then, and only then, will we find the proper balance that leads to true contentment.

## The Grace Adventure

11. You may want to close this study with a time of prayer. Take a moment for each group member to tell one thing God has impressed upon him or her during this study. Ask God to continue to mold your attitudes toward money and to show you new ways you can serve Him by giving your money and yourself.

## During the Week

- Review the verses you have focused on during this study. What has the Holy Spirit revealed in them that you didn't see when you started? If you haven't yet outlined a giving plan, decide on one today.

\*   \*   \*   \*

*"Seek first His kingdom and His righteousness; and all these things shall be added to you"* (Matthew 6:33).

Moody Press, a ministry of Moody Bible Institute, is designed for education, evangelization, and edification. If we may assist you in knowing more about Christ and the Christian life, please write us without obligation: Moody Press, c/o MLM, Chicago, Illinois 60610.